DID DINOSAURS LIVE IN YOUR BACKYARD?

Questions and Answers About Dinosaurs

MELVIN AND GILDA BERGER
ILLUSTRATED BY ALAN MALE

SCHOLASTIC REFERENCE

Contents

KEY TO ABBREVIATIONS
cm = centimeter/centimetre
g = gram
kg = kilogram
km = kilometer/kilometre
m = meter/metre
t= tonne

Text copyright © 1998 by Melvin and Gilda Berger
Illustrations copyright © 1998 by Alan Male
All rights reserved. Published by Scholastic Inc.
SCHOLASTIC and associated logos are trademarks and/or registered trademarks of Scholastic Inc.

No part of this publication may be reproduced, or stored in a retrieval system, or transmitted in any form or by any means, electronic, mechanical, photocopying, recording, or otherwise, without written permission of the publisher. For information regarding permission, write to Scholastic Inc., Attention: Permissions Department, 555 Broadway, New York, NY 10012.

LIBRARY OF CONGRESS CATALOGING-IN-PUBLICATION DATA
Berger, Melvin.
Did dinosaurs live in your backyard? / Melvin and Gilda Berger.
p. cm.
Summary: Questions and answers explore such topics as what the dinosaurs were, what they ate, what color they were, and how we know about them.
1. Dinosaurs—Miscellanea—Juvenile literature. [1. Dinosaurs—Miscellanea. 2. Fossils—Miscellanea. 3. Paleontology—Miscellanea. 4. Questions and answers.] I. Berger, Gilda. II. Title.
QE862.D5B4857   1998   567.9—dc21   97-30263   CIP   AC

ISBN 0-590-13078-1 (pob)
ISBN 0-439-08568-3 (pb)

Book design by David Saylor and Nancy Sabato

10 9 8 7 6 5 4 3 2 1   9/9 0/0 01 02

Printed in Mexico   49
First printing, August 1999

Expert Reader: Robert Asher, DPAS State University of New York, Stony Brook, NY

For Maxwell, amazing and curious
— M. AND G. BERGER

For Nina & Chloe
— A. MALE

Introduction

Why read a question-and-answer book?

Because you're a kid! And kids are curious.
It's natural—and important—to ask *questions* and look for *answers*.
This book answers many questions that you may have:

- Which was the first dinosaur?
- Did some dinosaurs have two brains?
- What color were the dinosaurs?
- Did dinosaurs have families?
- What happened to the dinosaurs?

Many of the answers will surprise and amaze you. We hope they'll tickle
your imagination. Maybe they will lead you to ask *more questions* calling for
more answers. That's what being curious is all about!

Melvin Berger   *Gilda Berger*

THE WORLD OF DINOSAURS

Did dinosaurs live in your backyard?

Probably. Dinosaurs lived all over the world. You can find dinosaur remains on every continent: North and South America, Asia, Europe, Africa, Australia, and even Antarctica.

In North America alone there are signs of dinosaur life everywhere. At least 28 states and the District of Columbia in the United States, six provinces in Canada, and parts of Mexico boast dinosaur remains. So—there's a good chance that dinosaurs lived in your backyard and walked where you walk today.

What are dinosaurs?

A large group of amazing animals that ruled the earth many millions of years ago. Dinosaurs came in all shapes and sizes. Among them were dinosaurs

- as tall as buildings.
- longer than tennis courts.
- faster than racehorses.
- armed with dagger-sharp teeth.
- heavier than railroad cars.

Dinosaurs are related to reptiles, such as crocodiles, lizards, snakes, and turtles. But dinosaurs also seem to be related to birds. What fascinating creatures they were!

When did the dinosaurs live?

During a period of Earth's history called the Mesozoic era, or "middle life." The Mesozoic lasted from about 225 million to 65 million years ago. Dinosaurs appeared near the beginning of the era. And they were gone by the end. That means the dinosaurs ruled the world for over 150 million years.

Compared to the dinosaurs, humans are newcomers on planet Earth. Our first ancestors appeared less than four million years ago!

Tyrannosaurus

How do we know about dinosaurs?

From fossils. Fossils are the remains or traces of animals or plants that lived long ago. Dinosaur bones, teeth, and eggs are fossils. So are the footsteps that dinosaurs left in mud.

Some dinosaurs fell into water or onto wetland after they died. Their bodies got covered by sand or soil. The flesh and skin of these dinosaurs rotted away. Over millions of years, the hard parts of their bodies changed into stone. These hard parts became fossils.

Who digs for fossils?

Scientists called paleontologists (pay-lee-on-TOL-uh-jists). These scientists are also known as fossil hunters.

Sometimes paleontologists find dinosaur bones lying on the ground or sticking out of a hill or cliff. They may uncover fossils by digging in places where they have already found bones. Or, farmers, miners, or others may come across fossils while digging in the earth. Someday you just might be lucky enough to spot a fossil yourself!

What do fossil bones and teeth tell us?

Lots! From dinosaur bones we learn the animal's size and weight. Long, heavy bones tell us the dinosaur was large. And teeth usually tell a story, too. The bigger the teeth, the bigger the animal.

Tooth shape helps us discover what dinosaurs ate. Meat eaters had long, sharp teeth for biting prey. The teeth of plant eaters were often shaped like pegs for pulling off leaves and fruit from trees.

Skulls reveal the size of the dinosaur's brain. Dinosaurs with big brains were probably smarter that those with small brains. Big eye sockets are a sign of good sight. And large nasal cavities usually mean a first-class sense of smell.

Why are fossil footprints important?

They can show the way the dinosaur walked and how fast. Most dinosaurs were good walkers, moving along briskly between 3 and 6 miles (5 and 10 km) an hour. They put one foot in front of another, much as we do.

Some dinosaurs could run fast. Their speed could top 20 miles (32 km) an hour—far faster than most humans.

Did dinosaurs walk on two feet or on four feet?

Early plant eaters walked either on two feet or on all fours—as apes do. But the giant plant eaters that came later almost always walked on four legs—more like elephants.

Most meat-eating dinosaurs walked upright on two hind legs. They held their long tails straight out behind them for balance. Many dinosaurs limped. Was it because of injuries? Or was it because they were carrying heavy loads, such as young dinosaurs? The answer may lie in the fossil footprints.

Did dinosaurs live alone or in groups?

Probably in groups. Fossil tracks of various meat-eating dinosaurs seem to show they lived and hunted in packs, much like wolves.

Some plant eaters also kept together in groups. Animals in packs were safer than animals living alone. Very young dinosaurs probably moved with the herd soon after birth.

Paleontologists sometimes find many dinosaur fossils close together. That may mean whole herds lived—and died—together.

Did all dinosaurs leave fossils?

No. Millions of dinosaurs died on dry land. Their flesh and their bones rotted away. They are gone without a trace. And millions more were eaten by their enemies—bones and all. Nothing is left of these dinosaurs, either.

Which dinosaur fossil was found first?

Iguanodon (ih-GWA-nuh-duhn), or "iguana tooth." In 1821,
Mary Ann Mantell was hunting fossils with her husband,
Gideon, a British doctor. She found a huge fossil tooth. Her
husband thought the tooth came from a giant iguana, which
he named *Iguanodon*. Much later, scientists decided it was
not an iguana at all. It was really the first dinosaur fossil ever
found!

Where were most *Iguanodon* fossils found?

Europe. The biggest find dates back to 1878. Miners in Belgium, digging
for coal deep beneath the ground, came upon hundreds of *Iguanodon*
remains. When put together like giant jigsaw puzzles, the bones formed 40
skeletons. They told a lot about *Iguanodon*—amazing creatures that lived
more than 100 million years ago.

What do we know about *Iguanodon*?

Iguanodon stood about 15 feet (5 m) high, was 30 feet (9 m) long, and weighed up to 10,000 pounds (4,500 kg). This large plant eater walked on all fours while grazing on low-growing vegetation. But when browsing on shrubs or defending itself against predators, *Iguanodon* might have used its front legs as hands. In any case, its footprints are 36 inches (91 cm) long. Try finding a shoe to fit that foot!

Who made up the name "dinosaur"?

The British scientist Richard Owen, in 1841. Owen was studying several large fossils. They looked like lizard bones. But they were much bigger. The bones were about the size of giant elephant bones.

Owen knew that no modern lizard grew that large. He decided the fossils must belong to a separate group of animals that had disappeared a long time ago. He named these animals *Dinosauria,* or "terrible lizards."

Of course, now we know that dinosaurs were not lizards at all, and only a few were terrible. But the name stuck.

How do dinosaurs get their names?

A couple of ways. The first person to find the fossil can give it a name that describes the dinosaur. For example, *Tyrannosaurus* means "tyrant lizard." Or, the name can be the place where the fossil was found. *Edmontosaurus* fossils originally came from around Edmonton, Canada. Still others are named after people. *Herrerasaurus* took its name from Victorino Herrera, the Argentine goatherd who first noticed the fossil.

Were dinosaurs cold-blooded or warm-blooded?

At first, paleontologists thought dinosaurs were cold-blooded, like lizards and other reptiles. Cold-blooded animals get heat from outside their bodies. When cold, they move more slowly. They warm up by basking in the sun. If they get too hot, they seek shade.

Later, experts thought some dinosaurs were warm-blooded, like birds and mammals. Warm-blooded animals produce heat inside their bodies. They can live in cold and hot climates. Their bodies have a rich blood supply.

Now we think some dinosaurs, like *Spinosaurus,* may have been cold-blooded, some warm-blooded, and others not fully one or the other.

Spinosaurus

How many different kinds of dinosaurs lived on Earth?

We know of about 350 kinds. There might have been more than 1,000 different types of dinosaurs. But no one's really sure.

Did any dinosaurs swim?

No. Dinosaurs lived on the land. Many waded in shallow water, but none could swim. *Ichthyosaurs* (IK-thee-uh-sawrs), or "fish lizards," were swimming creatures that lived at the same time as the dinosaurs. But *Ichthyosaurs* were not dinosaurs.

What else lived at the time of the dinosaurs?

Turtles, crocodiles, lizards, and later, birds and snakes lived alongside the dinosaurs. Many kinds of small mammals, as well as cockroaches as long as your forearm, scampered in the underbrush. Large flying insects, such as giant, 3-foot (1 m) dragonflies, whirred through the air. And sharks, starfish, and clams lived in the sea.

What color were the dinosaurs?

Probably many colors. From fossil skin impressions found in some rocks we know that the skin of some dinosaurs was scaly and bumpy—much like the skin of lizards. And each kind of dinosaur seemed to have its own pattern.

Today's lizards have stripes, spots, or patches of color to camouflage and protect them. Their bright hues also help attract a mate. Perhaps, then, dinosaurs also had colorful hides for the same reasons.

Oviraptor

How long did dinosaurs live?

Different lengths of time. The life span of a dinosaur was probably related to its size. Smaller dinosaurs may have reached adulthood quickly. Perhaps they lived five years or so. But giant ones could have lived far, far longer.

Some large reptiles of today, such as turtles, live for well over 100 years. With a little luck, dinosaurs could have lived at least that long.

How were baby dinosaurs born?

Most, if not all, hatched from eggs. Egg-laying dinosaurs made nests by scooping out mounds of dirt on high, dry ground. The nests were about the size of giant truck tires. Often the dinosaurs dug nests close together, with just enough room to move between them.

Dinosaurs laid eggs in the nests. Fossil hunters have found eggs that range in size from about 4 to 10 inches (10 to 25 cm).

Did mother dinosaurs sit on the eggs?

Mother dinosaurs probably didn't put all their weight on their eggs. They may have gently rested on top of them to keep the eggs warm.

Scientists once believed that *Oviraptor* (oh-vee-RAP-tuhr), or "egg stealer," swiped the eggs of dinosaurs like *Protoceratops* (proh-toh-SAIR-uh-tops), or "first horned face." Then paleontologists made two discoveries: an egg containing an unborn *Oviraptor* where they expected to find *Protoceratops* eggs, and the fossil of an adult female *Oviraptor* on top of a nest of eggs. Now they think *Oviraptor* was not an egg-stealer, at all. It probably warmed its own eggs, just as birds do today.

THE RISE OF DINOSAURS

What was the world like when dinosaurs first appeared?

The earliest dinosaurs date back to the first part of the Mesozoic era. It was called the Triassic period. The Triassic lasted from about 225 million to 200 million years ago.

At the start of the Triassic, all the continents were joined together in one giant landmass surrounded by ocean. The dinosaurs wandered freely over the vast stretches of land. Later, the land slowly began to break apart and form separate continents.

Turtles, crocodiles, insects, and snails were some of the animals who lived during the Triassic. Evergreen trees, ferns, and mosses grew everywhere in the hot, humid climate.

Which was the first dinosaur?

No one knows for sure. But *Herrerasaurus* (her-air-uh-SAWR-us), or "Herrera's lizard," was surely among the first to appear.

Herrerasaurus lived about 220 million years ago. At 6 to 8 feet (2 to 2.4 m) tall, *Herrerasaurus* weighed in at about 300 pounds (135 kg). It ran on two feet and used its sharp teeth and powerful jaws to catch and eat smaller animals. According to one expert, *Herrerasaurus* had teeth like a shark, claws like an eagle, a neck like an antelope, and a backside like an ostrich.

Were other dinosaurs around at the same time?

Eoraptor (ee-oh-RAP-tur), or "dawn stealer," was also active during the Triassic period. The bones of *Eoraptor* were found less than a mile (1.6 km) from those of *Herrerasaurus*.

   About the size of a dog, *Eoraptor* was 3 feet (1 m) long and weighed 25 pounds (11 kg). This fast, two-legged runner may have hunted or fed on dead animals.

Were early dinosaurs small?

Probably most Triassic dinosaurs were light in weight and small in size. It is also likely that they were meat eaters that walked on their hind legs.

What happened at the end of the Triassic period?

Many new kinds of dinosaurs began to appear. Some looked much like the early creatures. But others were big, heavy meat eaters that walked on two legs.

A few kinds of very large plant-eating dinosaurs began to show up, too. These new dinosaurs used all four legs for walking.

These are only some of the dinosaurs that lived on Earth.

Herrerasaurus

Therapsid

Nyasasaurus

Melanorosaurus

Thecodontosaurus

Plateosaurus

Brachiosaurus

Thotobolosaurus

Aetosaur

Lagosuchus

Coloradisaurus

Proterosuchian

Ischisaurus

Dolichosuchus

Diplodocus

Coelophysis

Staurikosaurus

Walkeria

Stegosaurus

TRIASSIC PERIOD

JURASSIC

What came after the Triassic period?

The Jurassic period, or second part of the Mesozoic era. It lasted from about 200 million to 135 million years ago. The big supercontinent continued to break apart into smaller continents. The climate stayed warm and moist. Plants spread across the land.

During this period, the first feathered birds took to the sky. Tiny, fur-covered mammals appeared. But most of all, the earth shook with the heavy footsteps of the biggest dinosaurs that ever lived.

Were all the Jurassic dinosaurs large?

No. *Compsognathus* (komp-so-NAY-thus), or "pretty jaw," was the size of a small chicken, but *Compsognathus* was far from cute. It ran fast on its two long, thin legs, its mouth wide open. Its teeth snapped up small animals and insects.

Pteranodon

Spinosaurus

Tyrannosaurus

Mamenchisaurus

Struthiomimus

Allosaur

Iguanadon

Torosaurus

Parasaurolophus

Kentrosaurus

Euoplocephalus

Baryonyx

Ornithomimus

Ornatotholus

Dilophosaurus

Xuanhanosaurus

PERIOD

CRETACEOUS PERIOD

Which were the largest dinosaurs?

Brachiosaurus (BRAK-ee-uh-sawr-us), or "arm lizard," and its relatives. Eighty feet (24 m) long, *Brachiosaurus* stretched nearly the full length of a basketball court. At 80 tons (81.3 t), it weighed as much as three fully loaded concrete mixers! Its 20-foot (6 m) shoulders were as high as a full-grown giraffe, and it had a 30-foot (9 m) neck that was half the length of a bowling alley. When craning its neck, *Brachiosaurus* stood 40 feet (12 m) tall—as high as a four-story building!

Scientists have found other Brachiosaurid bones from animals which were probably even bigger. Some may have been over 100 feet (30 m) long and weighed a staggering 130 tons (132 t)!

What did the biggest dinosaurs eat?

Plants—including the leaves, stems, fruit, seeds, twigs, and small branches. And eat they did! Each one gulped down as much as 1 ton (1.016 t) of food every day. That's what it took to fill the belly of these giant beasts!

The dinosaur sometimes clamped its mouth shut over a big branch. Then it pulled its head back—stripping the branch clean! This way of eating made deep scratch marks on dinosaur teeth. But what a quick, easy way to get a mouth full of leaves!

How did dinosaurs get new teeth?

They grew them. If a tooth became worn down or broken, a new one grew in to take its place. In fact, under each row of dinosaur teeth were several more rows. As the new teeth grew in they pushed the old ones out. And this went on and on. Too bad the dinosaurs lived in the days before tooth fairies!

Why did some plant eaters have very long necks?

To pluck the upper leaves from tall trees. Some dinosaurs could only eat ground plants and the leaves on low branches. But dinosaurs with long necks could get to places the others could not reach. They were like today's giraffes.

Apatosaurus (ah-pat-uh-SAWR-us), or "deceptive lizard," had a 20-foot-long (6 m) neck. That's the length of a full-sized car! With a neck this long, *Apatosaurus* could strip leaves from the topmost branches. It could also bend over to eat low-growing plants. Some think that the mighty *Apatosaurus* may even have pushed trees over to get leafy meals.

What's the difference between *Apatosaurus* and *Brontosaurus*?

None! In 1877, a fossil was dug up in Colorado and named *Apatosaurus*. Two years later, a similar fossil was found in Wyoming. It was called *Brontosaurus* (BRON-tuh-sawr-us), or "thunder lizard." *Apatosaurus* and *Brontosaurus* were considered two different kinds of dinosaurs.

Then, in 1975, paleontologists realized that *Apatosaurus* and *Brontosaurus* were the same dinosaur. Since *Apatosaurus* was found first, scientists decided to call all these dinosaurs *Apatosaurus*.

Which dinosaur had the longest neck?

Mamenchisaurus (mah-men-chee-SAWR-us), or "Mamenchi lizard." It was named after the place in China where it was found.

The neck of this dinosaur was an amazing 30 feet (9 m) long—about the length of a big bus. Experts think it waded into water and floated its head on the surface. That would make life easy. *Mamenchisaurus* merely stretched out and ate all the water plants it could reach.

It's hard to imagine how blood reached a dinosaur's head through its very long neck. Long-necked dinosaurs probably had a big, strong heart to do the job.

Kentrosaurus

How long were the longest dinosaurs?

Diplodocus (dih-PLOD-uh-kus), or "double beam," stretched nearly 90 feet (28 m) from the tip of its extremely tiny head to the end of its whiplike tail. It had a 26-foot (8 m) neck and a tail almost twice as long. If *Diplodocus* were to flop down across the net of a tennis court, 6 feet (2 m) of neck and 6 feet (2 m) of tail would hang over the baselines.

Lately two dinosaurs, probably related to *Diplodocus*, have been found. *Supersaurus* (soo-per-SAWR-us), or "beyond lizard," and *Seismosaurus* (syze-muh-SAWR-us), or "earthquake lizard," were over 100 feet (30 m) long and weighed at least 50 tons (51 t). Each looked like a long bridge resting on four heavy posts.

Did plant eaters chew their food?

Many did not. Some, like *Diplodocus*, had small, peglike teeth. They were good for pulling leaves off trees or eating small ground plants—but that's all. They couldn't chew the hundreds of pounds (kilograms) of food the dinosaurs ate every day. So nature gave these vegetarians another way to digest their food.

Early in life, the young plant eaters swallowed lots of small stones. The stones stayed in their stomachs. From then on, the stones ground and mashed the leaves and plants the dinosaurs swallowed. The stomach stones must have worked very well. Some plant eaters grew to be the largest of all land animals!

How did plant eaters protect themselves?

Some dinosaurs had powerful spiked tails. *Kentrosaurus* (KEN-truh-sawr-us), or "spiked lizard," was only about 15 feet (5 m) long and 1 ton (1.016 t) in weight. But could it brawl!

Long, sharp spikes lined its back and tail. At the tip of its tail were four extremely big, spearlike points. When attacked, *Kentrosaurus* swung its tail at the enemy. The deadly spikes stabbed deep into the flesh of the attacking animal. With them, *Kentrosaurus* could fight off dinosaurs many times its size.

Why did some dinosaurs have bony plates on their backs?

To keep warm or to cool off. *Stegosaurus* (steg-uh-SAWR-us), or "lizard with a roof," had about 20 hard 2-foot-tall (60 cm) plates sticking up from its spine.

Like other cold-blooded animals, *Stegosaurus*'s body temperature changed with the weather. But the plates helped *Stegosaurus* stay comfortable.

On cold days, the dinosaur turned so that the sun struck the plates. This warmed the blood flowing through the plates and heated its body. On hot days, *Stegosaurus* moved so the plates were in the shade or caught the wind. That brought down its temperature.

Were dinosaurs smart?

Not very. Most dinosaurs had small brains compared to their body size. They would be dummies next to today's dogs or cats. Scientists believe that *Stegosaurus* had the smallest brain for its size of any dinosaur. This giant plant eater could weigh 2 tons (2t), yet its brain was tiny and weighed only a few ounces (grams).

Did some dinosaurs have two brains?

Perhaps. Take *Tuojiangosaurus* (twah-JEEAHNG-uh-sawr-us), or "Tuojiang lizard," for example. It was named after the river in China where it was found. *Tuojiangosaurus* had a big bump on its spine, just over its hips. The bulge was 20 times bigger than its small brain.

Today, scientists think the bump is where nerves from the back half of the dinosaur's body linked up with the spine. In an animal, the nerves connect with its brain. So many say *Tuojiangosaurus* had a second brain.

Which Jurassic dinosaur fed on most other dinosaurs?

Allosaurus (AL-uh-sawr-us), or "strange lizard." What a monster it was, with a huge skull, great, gaping jaws, and 3-inch-long (7.6 cm) teeth! Some *Apatosaurus* fossils have tooth marks of *Allosaurus* on them. This suggests that *Allosaurus* was the killer.

THE TRIUMPH OF DINOSAURS

Which was the last part of the Mesozoic era?

The Cretaceous period, from about 135 million to 65 million years ago. The continents were becoming more like they are today. Warm, shallow seas covered half of the continent of North America.

Birds, mammals, insects, and sea creatures continued to grow and develop. Flowering plants and several kinds of trees started to grow. During this period, too, some spectacular dinosaurs appeared, including the mighty *Tyrannosaurus*.

How did Cretaceous dinosaurs protect themselves?

Some were built like army tanks. Plates of stiff, strong bone covered the backs of dinosaurs, such as *Ankylosaurus* (ang-KILE-uh-sawr-us), or "stiff lizard." This "armor" helped them fend off attacking meat eaters. Even their eyelids had armor. Shutting their eyes was like slamming down metal blinds.

Did any dinosaur have armor all over its body?

Saichania (SYE-kahn-ee-uh), or "beautiful one," did. This dinosaur had armor everywhere—even over its stomach. And its coat of armor was covered with knobs and spikes for added protection.

Was *Ankylosaurus* heavy and slow-moving?

Heavy? Yes. Slow-moving? Perhaps not always.
Scientists think *Ankylosaurus* may have run as fast as
a modern rhinoceros—up to 25 miles (40 km) an
hour—in a short spurt.

Which dinosaur had three horns?

Triceratops (try-SAIR-uh-tops), or "face with three horns." The two horns over its eyes were long and sharp. Each one measured more than 3 feet (1 m)! A shorter and more blunt horn stuck up from its nose. When in danger, *Triceratops* aimed the spearlike horns at its enemy. Then—watch out—it charged forward at up to 25 miles (40 km) an hour!

Triceratops's skull was 7 feet (2 m) long, which is more than ten times the size of your skull. At an amazing 2,000 pounds (900 kg), the head weighed as much as an ox.

Did any dinosaur carry a club?

Euoplocephalus (you-oh-plo-SEF-uh-luhs), or "well-armored head." Its name comes from its thick head covering. But *Euoplocephalus* is best known for the big, bony club at the tip of its rather long tail.

Suppose an enemy bent over to take a bite. *Euoplocephalus* would swing its tail and smash the attacker's face. If that didn't do the trick, *Euoplocephalus* could break the enemy's leg with one swat of its club.

Which dinosaur had the biggest head?

Torosaurus (TOR-uh-sawr-us), or "bull lizard." In fact, *Torosaurus* had the biggest head of all known land animals. Its mammoth head was about 9 feet (3 m) long—the size of a small car.

Torosaurus also had an amazing, 5 1/2-foot-wide (almost 2 m), bony shield at the back of the head. This structure is called a frill. The frill extended over most of the creature's back. Scientists believe that the wide frill helped *Torosaurus* hold up its swelled head.

Why are some dinosaurs called "bone heads"?

Because their skull had a 9-inch (23 cm) layer of bone! *Pachycephalosaurus* (pak-ee-sef-uh-luh-SAWR-us), or "thick-headed lizard," was the biggest "bone head" of all. This dinosaur always looked as if it were wearing a huge crash helmet.

But don't think *Pachycephalosaurus* used its big head only to protect itself. The bony layer also helped the dinosaur battle others in the herd. *Pachycephalosaurus* probably butted heads like today's goats. The reason may have been the same: to become leader of the group or to win a mate.

Did dinosaurs have families?

Some kinds surely did. Plant eaters named *Maiasaura* (my-uh-SAWR-uh), or "good mother lizard," are a good example. Remains of the 30-foot-long (9 m) dinosaurs showed up near a cluster of nests they had dug in the ground.

The 2-foot-deep (60 cm) and 7-foot-wide (2 m) nests held smashed bits of eggshell. This told scientists that the young stayed in the nest for a long time. Most likely the parents fed them by mouth—just like baby birds are fed—until they were strong enough to leave the nest.

Around the nests were fossils of 15 young *Maiasaura*, ranging in size from 3 to 15 feet (1 to 5 m). Some paleontologists think the family cared for the young until they were nearly grown.

Did *any* plant eaters chew their food?

Several Cretaceous plant eaters did chew their food. This included the duckbills, or *Hadrosaurs*. The best-known duckbill is *Edmontosaurus* (ed-MON-tuh-sawr-us), or "Edmonton lizard."

Edmontosaurus had about 1,000 teeth! They are often called "cheek teeth" because they were set so far back in the mouth. The teeth were cemented together in four rows of a few hundred each. The top and bottom rows rubbed against each other like big, rough files when *Edmontosaurus* ate. Together they did a great job of crushing and grinding leaves.

Maiasaura

What sounds did the duckbills make?

Probably loud honks and barks. *Parasaurolophus* (par-uh-saur-uh-LOAF-us), or "similar crested lizard," had a 4-foot (120 cm) crest on top of its head. Inside the crest was a hollow tube more than 3 feet (1 m) long. Some think that when *Parasaurolophus* breathed out strongly, the tube made a loud honking sound, something like a modern trombone.

The long snout on *Edmontosaurus* may have been covered with loose skin. It might have looked like the nose on today's elephant seal. The similarity makes experts think that *Edmontosaurus* may have barked like its look-alike.

Why did some dinosaurs have huge sails?

For heating and air-conditioning, just like the plates on *Stegosaurus*. The "sail" on *Spinosaurus* (SPY-nuh-sawr-us), or "spiny lizard," stuck up over its back, like the sail on a sailboat. It was held up by long, thin bones attached to the dinosaur's spine.

The sail kept *Spinosaurus* comfortable. When cold, the dinosaur heated its sail in the sun's rays. That warmed its whole body. When too hot, the dinosaur moved so the sail was in the shade or picked up a breeze. What a really cool idea!

Were there more meat eaters or plant eaters?

Plant eaters. For every kind of meat-eating dinosaur, there might have been as many as 10 to 20 kinds of plant eaters.

How were meat eaters alike?

Meat eaters either preyed on other dinosaurs or on different kinds of animals. Most had a large mouth and overly large teeth in proportion to its head.

Meat eaters were also alike in other ways. All walked on two hind legs. They had streamlined bodies that were good for chasing their prey. Their arms were usually small, and their fingers were tipped with very large, catlike claws.

Which dinosaur is the most famous meat eater?

Tyrannosaurus (tye-RAN-uh-SAWR-us), or "tyrant lizard." A full-grown, 20-foot-long (6 m) *Tyrannosaurus* was taller than a telephone pole. If you had lived in the Age of Dinosaurs, you barely would have reached as high as its knee. Most *Tyrannosaurus* fossils have been found in North America.

This giant, pea-brained meat eater grew to be 40 feet (12 m) long from snout to tail. A 7-ton (7.1 t) body made it far heavier than an elephant. Its huge head held about 60 incredibly sharp teeth—each as long as a steak knife!

Were any meat eaters bigger than *Tyrannosaurus*?

Perhaps. A lone fossil of *Giganotosaurus* (jye-gan-uh-tuh-SAWR-us), or "giant lizard," from South America is a little larger than *Tyrannosaurus*. Another single dinosaur found in Africa, *Carcharodontosaurus* (kar-char-h-DON-tuh-SAWR-us), or "shark-toothed lizard," also seems to top *Tyrannosaurus* in size.

More fossils need to be found before we'll know for sure if the average *Giganotosaurus* or *Carcharodontosaurus* was bigger than *Tyrannosaurus*. Scientists may also learn if these giant beasts hunted prey or ate dead animals.

Did dinosaurs have claws?

Most of them did. But the most frightening ones belonged to *Deinonychus* (dye-NON-ik-us), or "terrible claw." This dinosaur was only 12 feet (3.6 m) long. But it had a pair of unusually long, strong arms with three-fingered hands. Each finger ended in a curved, hook-shaped claw.

But one "terrible claw" gave the dinosaur its name. Five inches (1.3 cm) long, sickle-shaped, and sharply pointed, it stood out above the other foot claws. *Deinonychus* flung itself against an enemy, with feet raised. Then the terrible claw slashed open the victim's belly—like a knife slicing through meat.

What sounds did the meat eaters make?

The largest meat-eating dinosaurs probably roared like modern lions. These dinosaurs had gigantic skulls. Some think that the skulls added loudness to their calls. No doubt the sound boomed out over long distances.

Were meat eaters smarter than plant eaters?

Yes. To be a good hunter, an animal needs sharper senses, faster reflexes, and greater speed than a grazing animal.

Troödon (TROH-uh-don), or "wound tooth," was probably the smartest of the dinosaurs. A small, birdlike beast, Troödon had the largest brain for its size. Big eyes and long, sharp claws on fingers and toes made it fit for catching the small, scurrying animals Troödon liked to eat.

Which was the fastest of all dinosaurs?

Struthiomimus (strooth-ee-oh-MY-muss), or "like an ostrich." Struthiomimus could easily reach speeds of about 50 miles (80 km) an hour—faster than a racehorse. At this breakneck speed, Struthiomimus had no trouble catching its dinner of insects and small animals.

Struthiomimus was named after the ostrich for good reasons. Standing 8 feet (240 cm) tall, it was the size of a modern ostrich. Like the ostrich, Struthiomimus had large eyes, a horny, birdlike beak, and no teeth. But here the similarity ends. What kind of ostrich has scaly skin, a long tail, and two short arms?

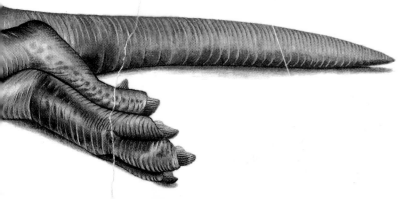

THE END OF DINOSAURS

What happened to dinosaurs toward the end of the Cretaceous period?

Three-fourths of all dinosaurs died out. In the last 10 million years of the Cretaceous, nearly three out of every four kinds of dinosaurs disappeared. By the end of the Cretaceous, 65 million years ago, the dinosaurs were practically all gone. They had become extinct.

Why did the dinosaurs become extinct?

Scientists have a few theories. One is that Earth grew very cold at the end of the Cretaceous. It was like winter all the time. The frigid air made the dinosaurs very cold. Keeping warm and finding food became very difficult. The dinosaurs weakened and died.

Another theory is that a star exploded in the sky. It sent out powerful cosmic rays. The deadly rays killed off many dinosaurs. They soon vanished.

The most popular theory is that a blazing asteroid from outer space smashed into Earth. The explosion of that asteroid brought the Age of Dinosaurs to a close.

How could one asteroid kill all the dinosaurs?

The asteroid was a 9-mile-wide (14.4 km) hunk of rock. It struck Earth near modern-day Mexico with terrific force. The impact caused a gigantic explosion—perhaps the greatest on Earth. The blast sent up an enormous cloud of dust, including soil, ash, rock, and hot steam. The cloud billowed into the air. Winds spread the thick, dark dust everywhere.

The dust blotted out the sun for many months. Plants dried up and died. Without food to eat, the plant-eating dinosaurs could not live. Without dinosaurs to prey on, the meat-eating dinosaurs also starved to death. Before long, the dinosaurs were gone.

Did other animals survive the asteroid?

Many birds, frogs, turtles, crocodiles, cockroaches, and, of course, mammals lived through the asteroid crash. Most survivors were smaller than the dinosaurs. Some may have hidden underwater or in burrows under the ground. Others may have needed very little food. The real reason some survived and others died out is still a question.

Why do we think an asteroid crashed into Earth?

Two reasons. Scientists found lots of iridium in Earth rocks that are 65 million years old. Iridium is a very rare chemical element on Earth. But it is common in asteroids and other bodies in space. The element could have been brought here by an asteroid at the end of the Cretaceous period.

Also, there is a crater—nearly 200 miles (320 km) across—on the coast of modern Mexico. Half is on the tip of the Yucatán Peninsula, and half is in the Gulf of Mexico. This big hole is now covered over by dirt and water. But it appears to have been made by an asteroid that fell to Earth 65 million years ago—the time the iridium layer was set down!

Why do scientists think dinosaurs and birds are related?

Because some fossils show dinosaur and bird features.

Archaeopteryx (ar-kee-OP-tuh-riks), or "ancient wing," was a pigeon-sized creature with dinosaur bones and teeth. Yet *Archaeopteryx* also had feathers and wings. It seemed to be part dinosaur, part bird.

Mononykus (ma-no-NY-kus), or "one elbow claw," was the size of a turkey. Its bones were like those of a bird and it may have been covered with feathers. But, like some dinosaurs, it had a mouth full of sharp teeth and a long tail. Was *Mononykus* a bird or a dinosaur? Very likely, it was both!

Are we still discovering dinosaurs?

Yes. Scientists find about seven new kinds of dinosaurs every year. And each discovery teaches us more about the fascinating world of the dinosaurs.

Recently, paleontologists found a birdlike dinosaur fossil in China. The fossil included the dinosaur's internal organs. For the first time, scientists could actually see these parts of a dinosaur.

Other paleontologists noticed a mammal's bones inside the remains of a dinosaur. It seems the dinosaur had eaten the mammal just before dying. This gave the first proof that dinosaurs ate mammals.

Do we have more to learn about dinosaurs?

Yes, from "Where did dinosaurs come from?" to "Why did dinosaurs survive so long?"—and lots of questions in between!

At this moment scientists around the world are looking for dinosaur fossils. And thousands of remains await study in museums and laboratories. Perhaps the greatest dinosaur discoveries are yet to be made.

Will dinosaurs live in my backyard again?

No. Dinosaurs are gone forever. No animal that became extinct has ever returned.

This leaves us with two thoughts. One is to work to save the many living animals and plants that are in danger of becoming extinct today. Don't let the tiger, elephant, and blue whale go the way of the dinosaurs.

The other is to be thankful that the dinosaurs once graced our planet. They are a glorious and exciting part of our past.

Index

Page numbers in bold indicate illustrations.

About the Authors

As kids growing up in New York City, the Bergers frequented the dinosaur exhibits at the fantastic American Museum of Natural History. As parents, they introduced their children to the exciting world of dinosaurs. As writers, they've visited the museum's labs and spoken with leading paleontologists. Now they share what they've learned with you.

About the Illustrator

Alan Male lives in England. He has worked as an artist for twenty-five years. Mr. Male likes to draw animals, plants, people, and landscapes. "The thing I like best about drawing dinosaurs is recreating animals that don't exist anymore," he says.